Khristina,

God, Country, True Stories
...and a Bunch of Nonsense in Rhyme

By Karen Swanson

God bless you,

Karen Swanson

10-29-05

ISBN: 1-4107-2446-8 (e-book)
ISBN: 1-4107-2447-6 (Paperback)

This book is printed on acid free paper.

1stBooks – rev. 05/16/03

To my husband, Don; my children, Lori, Mike, and Mindy; and my godchild, Troy.

A Table of Contents

PART ONE: Nonsense

When Off Is Off 3
Me Overweight? 5
I Got Myself a Little Dog 7
Watch Your Intake 9
Bad Breath Blues 11
My Dog Baxter Can Talk 13
Bare Hair Care 15
Full Coverage 17
Duh! 19
Breaking a Child Into Winter 21
Don't Blame the Holidays 23
One Holer Paperwork 25
You'll Know It's a Lawyer If... 27
Me Not Like Your Relatives? 29
The Fruit that Doesn't Lie 31
Catch-22 33
Class Reunion 35
Old Age — Not What it's Cracked Up to Be 37
No Smoking Please 39

PART TWO: True Stories

I Say Call it Like it Is 43
Soggy Doggie 45
I Was Framed – Honest 47
A Farmgirl? NOT 49
Rainbow Ringlets 51
Possibly the Oldest Thing in the Store 53
Just Following Directions 55
Donald Goes Home 57
Sibling School Dropout 59
Doubling Your Money at Seven 61

Please Speak Clearly Nurse 63
Misspelled Catastrophe..65

PART THREE: God and Country

Body Piercing Saved My Life 69
It Was the Ultimate Love 71
Doubly Blest American...73
If You Say You're a Christian 75
Don't You Think It's Time We Honor Our Vietnam Vets?........77
One Year After 9-11 79
You Can Start Over...81
The Sanctity of Life 83
What is a Veteran – A Veteran's Day Tribute.........................85
Lord I Thank You for My Child...87
Thank You God for America..89

PART ONE
Nonsense

Karen Swanson

When Off Is Off

I can see it must confuse little kids
It's no wonder some are withdrawn
Why we say the buzzer or alarm went off
When in reality — they go on

Karen Swanson

Me Overweight?

Some folks might think I'm overweight
Not to worry — that's their call
I don't think of myself as overweight
Just a few feet undertall

Karen Swanson

I Got Myself a Little Dog

I got myself a little dog
He's as cute as he can be
He likes it when I rub his ears
And I know that he likes me

He doesn't have a pedigree
I guess he's just a mutt
What kind of breed I'd call him
It's your guess – who knows what

There is nothing fancy about him
But he's the perfect dog I know
Even if he couldn't win a ribbon
At any kind of show

I thought I'd give him a simple name
Nothing as simple as Sue
I decided to call him Fido
Spelled P H I D E A U

Karen Swanson

Watch Your Intake

One thing you teach kids from early on
Because it's something they won't know
It's okay to catch snowflakes on your tongue
But never eat yellow snow

Karen Swanson

Bad Breath Blues

Smokin' and chewin'
It ain't purty
In fact – if you ask me
It's downright dirty

It makes your teeth
Either brown or yeller
And makes it doggone hard
To get a feller

So if you're really lookin'
For a husband or a wife
Keep away from smokes and chews
And have better breath for life

Karen Swanson

My Dog Baxter Can Talk

My dog Baxter is very smart
And can answer any question you ask
How many dogs do you know that talk?
It's really quite a task

I asked him where you'd find a chimney
He hesitated and then muttered oof
Then he perked up his ears – cocked his head
And proudly he said roof

I asked who was the greatest baseball player
You won't believe it, but this is the truth
He perked up his ears – cocked his head
And proudly he said Ruth

I asked him what covered the trunk of a tree
You'll never guess his remark
He perked up his ears – cocked his head
And proudly he said bark

I asked him to describe his girlfriend
A cute little French Poodle named Bough
He perked up his ears – cocked his head
And proudly said Bough wow!

I asked him what sandpaper feels like
He sometimes likes to act tough
He perked up his ears – cocked his head
And proudly he said rough

Karen Swanson

Bare Hair Care

A bald man went into a store
To buy himself a comb
He knew he'd never part with it
So he just went right on home

Karen Swanson

Full Coverage

What do you get for someone
When there is nothing they haven't got
It's really a simple answer
A Penicillin shot

Karen Swanson

Duh!

A farmer had two horses
Their names were King and Cole
He could not tell the two apart
To save his living soul

They were both exactly the same height
And both the same weight, too
The hair in their manes was the same length
And both had eyes of blue

One day as he was plowing behind the horses
He saw something in his sights
He noticed that the tail on the black horse
Was a half inch longer than the white's

Karen Swanson

Breaking a Child Into Winter

Winter can become real bitter
And it really takes its toll
You haven't experienced winter until
You've stuck your tongue to a pole

Karen Swanson

Don't Blame the Holidays

The holidays are a fattening time
At least that's what I remember
Eating from Christmas to New Year's isn't the worst
It's from January to December

Karen Swanson

One Holer Paperwork
(Explained by a very senior citizen)

What's so great about toilet paper?
The Sears catalog worked just fine
It may not have been as soft
Some folks just have to whine

I know the catalogs are harder to get
But what is there to prove
I'll admit – that new fangled paper
Is easier to get in the groove

Karen Swanson

You'll Know It's a Lawyer If...

I once saw a bunch of lawyers
On a ship in the middle of the ocean
How do I know that they were lawyers?
Their lips were all in motion

Karen Swanson

Me Not Like Your Relatives?

What do you mean I don't like your relatives
For the most part I think they're just fine
It so happens that I like your mother-in-law
A whole lot better than mine

Karen Swanson

The Fruit that Doesn't Lie

Bananas are the perfect fruit
You don't have to guess what's inside
You'll know exactly what to expect
By looking at the hide

Most fruits are misleading
They might look beautiful to the eye
But the inside might be hard or mushy
Too woody, sour or dry

An apple can be too tart
The inside could be bruised and brown
As well as pears, peaches and apricots
If they fall on the ground

You know what bananas will taste like
Or when it is time to make bread or pie
You'll never be tricked or fooled because
It's the one fruit that doesn't lie

Karen Swanson

Catch-22

I was recently given barbells
I got them as a gift
How can I lift to get strong
When I'm not strong enough to lift?

Karen Swanson

Class Reunion

When your classmate shows up with a gorgeous blonde
And a long golden Cadillac undented
Before you get your nose out of joint
Keep in mind that they both might be rented

Karen Swanson

Old Age — Not What it's Cracked Up to Be

Old age is not what it's cracked up to be
It has its valleys and peaks
And every opening in your body
Either makes a noise or leaks

Karen Swanson

No Smoking Please

No smoking in this establishment
Is the majority's desire
So if you're smoking in this place
You'd better be on fire

Karen Swanson

PART TWO
True Stories

Karen Swanson

I Say Call it Like it Is

While in the hospital having had my last child
I was moved by their care — free of stress
Mid-morning a nurse asked if I'd like a doughnut
You better believe I said yes

For forty five minutes I anguished
Wondering what kind of doughnut would it be
Would it be frosted, glazed or have sprinkles?
I would just have to wait and see

An hour and a half had finally gone by
I was starting to feel underfed
When the same nurse popped into the room
And threw an inner tube on my bed

Karen Swanson

Soggy Doggie

How did Sam's tail get all wet?
A mother asked her son Tommy
He answered with guilt all over his face
I didn't suck Sam's tail, Mommy

Karen Swanson

I Was Framed – Honest

Have you entered an empty elevator
As the door is closing behind you
And you realize there is a smell
And not a good one, mind you
The elevator goes down one floor
And then it opens up
Then six people come aboard
You know what they're thinking, yup
They'd look at each other – then look at me
Didn't have to guess – what'd they think
It did not smell good – but there we stood
In somebody else's stink

Karen Swanson

A Farmgirl? NOT

My husband tried to teach me
How to disk the beans and corn
So he wouldn't have to work so late
And get up so early in the morn

For some reason he said it wasn't working out
But really I think I know
He didn't like me putting the blinkers on
At the end of every row

Karen Swanson

Rainbow Ringlets

I will often color my hair
And it's always quite a surprise
I never know what color my hair will be
Until the darn stuff dries

Karen Swanson

Possibly the Oldest Thing in the Store

I overheard two ladies
In an antique store one day
They were each pushing 90 years of age
And both heads were silver and gray

The one picked up a candy dish
And whispered loudly to her friend Louise
Why – this is no antique
My Grandmother had one of these

Karen Swanson

Just Following Directions

I drove to a fast food drive thru
And the speaker said one moment please
So we waited a good 5 minutes
All I wanted was a lemon freeze

She finally came back and said "go ahead"
So that's just what I did
I drove the minivan forward a ways
My teen was so embarrassed – she hid

Karen Swanson

Donald Goes Home

My friend was in the hospital
After having her second son
She thought she'd enjoy the rest
But she wasn't having much fun

She was very close to the nursery
And she couldn't stand the one baby's cry
She said it sounded like a duck
Her tolerance was not very high

She said to her husband – Please take us home
I can't stand it another minute
That duck in there is driving me crazy
Staying longer – my heart's just not in it

So they checked out – The three of them left
Getting out of there was a good stroke of luck
On the way home the baby started to cry
Who'd have guessed? – They brought home the duck

Karen Swanson

Sibling School Dropout

My best friend's grandchild was four-years-old
And her mother was expecting a baby
So they decided to send her to a sibling class
So she could adjust to the competition, maybe

The little brother was born and came home
He was checked out good by his sister
The mom tried to give her some attention
So she reached over the baby and kissed her

The sister still wasn't to sure about him
And asked her mom – where will he stay?
With us mom said – no really said sis
The class money's down the drain I would say

Karen Swanson

Doubling Your Money at Seven

My nephew was quite an entrepreneur
He liked when his teeth fell out
The tooth fairy would give him a dollar a tooth
A good stroke of business, no doubt

But he figured out all by himself
How to double the money he'd made
He could pull his little brother's teeth
Then just wait around to get paid

Karen Swanson

Please Speak Clearly Nurse

Have you ever been in a doctor's office
And had your vitals taken by the nurse
And as she rushes out of the room
I don't think there's anything worse

She mumbles something as she closes the door
And it's rare when I've heard what she's said
I never know if I should be stripping down
Or if she's checking my teeth instead

Karen Swanson

Misspelled Catastrophe

We received many beautiful gifts
At our wedding in '64
Lots of pretty pillowcases
And sheets and blankets galore

We were given a mixer and blender
And one of the shiniest toasters
Two tablecloths and nine lamps
And eight wooden butterfly coasters

I wrote thank-you notes for many days
No spare moment went to waste
Some got thanked for the wrong gifts
When their wedding cards got misplaced

But the most embarrassing part of all
Wasn't thanking the wrong one for towels
It was adding an "e" to the word bowl
And thanking twelve guests for bowels

Karen Swanson

PART THREE
God and Country

Karen Swanson

Body Piercing Saved My Life

Body piercing isn't something new
It's been going on for years
And up until the last few decades
It usually involved the ears

But body piercing saved my life
On a cross at Calvary
He stretched his arms wide — bowed his head and died
And he did it for you and me

Karen Swanson

It Was the Ultimate Love

If not for the Christ Child
There'd be no Christmas season
It was part of God's plan
To forgive sinful man
For a very good reason
Born of a virgin — conceived from above
God sent his own Son — our victory won
It was the ultimate love

His birth was quite humble
As He was laid in a manger
Many would come
He was worshipped by some
But to others a stranger
Shepherds and wise men — followed him from afar
They were guided for days — singing His praise
By a bright shining star

So go ahead hang that tinsel — so shiny
Put bulbs all over the tree
String hundreds of lights — red — green — blue and white
For the whole world to see
Just remember the Christ Child
Who was sent from our Father above
The best celebration is our gift of salvation
It was the ultimate love

Karen Swanson

Doubly Blest American

I was born in a small Midwest town
In this great U S of A
Don't know why I was so fortunate
But I thank God every day
I feel like I've been doubly blest
Calling home this land so free
I thank God that I'm an American
And for my eternity

When Jesus died, was crucified
His death changed everything
That unselfish act was Heavenly backed
He's my savior, Lord and King
I'm a Christian first and an American
That combo tops the rest
I've got the best of both worlds
I've been truly doubly blest

I could have been raised in a country
With no freedom in my life
Or watched my family die from
Lack of food — war and strife
I thank God I'm in America
Which I proudly call my home
You'll find no country like it
No matter where you roam

Karen Swanson

If You Say You're a Christian

If you say you're a Christian
And do not love your brother
The message is clear from God
We should love one another
Any act or word or deed
By which we knowingly disobey
We sin against God and man
Thank God we can pray

For God is forgiving
If we confess we've done wrong
That we all are sinners
And want to keep our faith strong
He lets us start over
How far does forgiveness go
He'll wipe away all of our sins
And make them whiter than snow

Karen Swanson

Don't You Think It's Time We Honor Our Vietnam Vets?

From counties across America
There are thousands nationwide
Men and women served our country
Many fought and many died
When Uncle Sam declared I need you
Many answered with no regrets
Don't you think it's time we honor
Our Vietnam vets?

Many a young man left his family
Getting big hugs from Dad and Mom
Most of them not even knowing
What or where was Vietnam
But they went willingly to serve us
As patriotic as it gets
Don't you think it's time we honor
Our Vietnam vets?

They didn't all want to be there
But they went just the same
They did not desert their country
No reason for guilt or shame
They went willingly and proudly
Like dads and granddads long before
And it's never ever easy
When you're going off to war

I thank you as an American
For serving there for me
And for helping keep our country
The land of the free
They built the wall of those who perished
Lest our country forget
But don't you think it's time we honor
All our Vietnam vets?

Thank you God for America
And for our Vietnam vets

One Year After 9-11

It's been more than a year now Lord
And what a year it has been
It's still one of disbelief
We agonize again and again

We found out first hand what terrorism is
And that we should be more on guard
We've seen what total devastation looks like
Right in our own back yard

It tends to make us less trusting
And more wary of the neighbor next door
One thing that is for certain
Things won't be as they were before

But we are more patriotic
We know what it is to be free
Waving our flags proudly and higher
For all the world to see

Karen Swanson

You Can Start Over

Do you feel troubled
With how your life has been?
Do things overpower you?
Wish you could start again?

Take the control back
With God's help it's true
You can start over
Make your life fresh and new

Has your life overwhelmed you?
Do you feel guilt and shame?
Do you think you've lost control
And you know you are to blame?

You can start over
It doesn't matter what you've done
You can start over
You've been forgiven through God's Son

You can start over
You can start anew
God has the answer
He's there for me and you

anson

The Sanctity of Life

The birth of a baby
Is a gift from above
A miracle of God
Most conceived out of love
A baby is precious
And loved and adored
The most precious baby
Was Jesus our Lord

Some think a life
Can be less than worthwhile
Wrong timing, sex or color
Can wreck a lifestyle
Too sick or too handicapped
Or too low an IQ
The sacredness of life
Does it matter to you?

All lives are cheapened
When we don't value each one
Life was sanctified
When God sent us His Son
The unborn and aged
Are important to man
God loves them all
It's part of His plan

The world is in trouble
If we don't stop to see
The sacredness of life
In each nationality
If we don't change our thinking
And put an end to this strife
It's just a matter of time

Until there's no sanctity of life

Thank you God for Your Son
And for the sanctity of life

What is a Veteran – A Veteran's Day Tribute

Webster defines a veteran as
A person who has served in any way
In the armed forces for our country
That's why we have Veteran's Day

Veteran's Day was first called Armistice Day
Which we celebrate the 11th of November
Honoring Veterans of both war and peacetime
Each and every armed forces member

A Veteran is very unselfish
Willing to lay his life on the line
Helping insure freedom for millions
Including families like yours and mine

We honor today all American vets
Who have answered our country's call
Including POWs and MIAs
Men and women giving their all

Our country would not be the country it is
If not for our soldiers so brave
Who left families behind to go to war
Helping our great nation to save

Your willingness to serve us
So faithfully day after day
Has made us all proud Americans
In this great U S of A

No thank you is ever big enough
To express how thankful we are
That you were so willing to fight for us
In places both near and far

Karen Swanson

As Americans we'd like to thank you
Each in our own special way
Please know you are not forgotten
But you're in our prayers everyday

Lord I Thank You for My Child

You were just a tiny baby
Seems like only yesterday
It's hard to imagine
How the time slipped away
But we loved you then
In a proud parent way
We never stopped loving
We love you more every day

When you went to school
Every day brought new things
You made lots of little friends
And kept spreading your wings
You loved Sunday School and T-ball
And basketball as well
You loved Grampa and Gramma
The piano—and show and tell

Your teen years got busy
And your homework increased
You took on many projects
Not slowing down in the least
Then you got your driver's license
Things weren't like they were before
You no longer needed mother
To get around anymore

We were not perfect parents
We had no textbooks that I recall
But you've become a special person
In spite of it all
I thank God everyday
For his love undefiled
Thank you God for your Son
And Lord I thank you for my child

Karen Swanson

Thank You God for America

It's hard for us to understand
How some can be filled with such hate
The magnitude boggles one's mind
It's real hard for us to relate

If they meant to destroy our country
They couldn't have been more wrong
It brought us all closer together
Our people are compassionate and strong

September 11th will never be the same
How ironic the date — nine one one
Many thousands of people lost loved ones
Each was someone's daughter or son

To lose several thousand people
Is a nightmare for one — just to hear it
Affecting hundreds of thousands of lives
They didn't win — nor did they break our spirit

We're experiencing many emotions
Including grief, anguish and fear
We know we will never forget it
But one thing is perfectly clear

We're very proud to be Americans
And when together as a free people, we're strong
We will rise like the Phoenix from the ashes
Because America is where we belong

Americans have never stood taller
Or risen more to the occasion
These people will not have died in vain
By these cowardly acts of invasion

Karen Swanson

We've heard about so many heroes
Helping out — their ultimate reaction
All the missing firemen, policemen and medics
Give new meaning to "missing in action"

This is where our God comes in
Testing the strength of our faith like none other
He is always there to comfort us
One more caring — there is not another

We need to pray for the victim's families
Their friends and co-workers too
And for all the search and rescue heroes
Some giving lives for ones they never knew

We need to pray for the survivors
Who are going through a lot
Including guilt that they survived
And many friends and co-workers did not

We need to pray for the innocent people
Who get caught up in the strife
And not judge all people by religion — because
Many lead a proud American life

We need to pray for our servicemen and women
Many on call and ready to leave
And the ones who've protected us all along
Are some of the finest, we believe

We need to pray for the leaders
From all countries — for what it's worth
Especially President Bush and our nation
The best country on this Earth

Our flag is where it belongs
Out for everyone to see
We're being reminded of the many who died
And what it means to be free

So the next time you think of freedom
And how we live it every day
Thank God for the men and women who've served
And for this great U S of A

About the Author

Karen Swanson was born and raised around North Branch, Minnesota. She is a homemaker and has three grown children. She stays busy with volunteer work, and enjoys flying with her husband and writing poetry.

Printed in the United States
1168300005B/313-627

You Can Start Over

Do you feel troubled
With how your life has been?
Do things overpower you?
Wish you could start again?

Take the control back
With God's help it's true
You can start over
Make your life fresh and new

Has your life overwhelmed you?
Do you feel guilt and shame?
Do you think you've lost control
And you know you are to blame?

You can start over
It doesn't matter what you've done
You can start over
You've been forgiven through God's Son

You can start over
You can start anew
God has the answer
He's there for me and you

Karen Swanson